# America at WAR

# Vietnam WAR

## TEN GREATEST BATTLES

### John Perritano

# Created by Q2AMedia
www.q2amedia.com

Text, design & illustrations Copyright © Leopard Learning 2012

**Editor** Jessica Cohn
**Project Manager** Shekhar Kapur
**Art Director** Joita Das
**Designers** Deepika Verma and Isha Khanna
**Picture Researchers** Akansha Srivastava and Nivisha Sinha

10 9 8 7 6 5 4 3 2 1

ISBN-13: 978-9-381-08701-5
ISBN: 9381087016

Printed in China

# Contents

# A Divisive War

The Vietnam War was the most divisive conflict in recent U.S. history. The war killed more than 58,000 U.S. soldiers and deeply divided the American people. It was the first war, some people say, which the United States did not win.

## Ousting the French

At one time, Vietnam was a French colony. During World War II (1939–1945), the Japanese conquered Vietnam. When the Allies defeated Japan, the French returned, but the Vietnamese did not want to be ruled by outsiders again. Vietnamese leader Ho Chi Minh and his **communist** followers—the Viet Minh—sought an independent Vietnam. They fought and defeated the French in a **guerilla** war.

## Divided in Two

However, freedom for the Vietnamese was elusive. The **Cold War** was beginning, and democratic countries were afraid of letting communists have total control of Vietnam. In 1954, international diplomats from Great Britain, France, the United States, and elsewhere split Vietnam in two. They allowed the communists to rule the North, while the South set up a democracy. In response, the Viet Minh decided to conquer South Vietnam. In the South, communists formed a pro-communist group called the **Viet Cong**.

**North and South Vietnam**

CHINA

NORTH VIETNAM

Hanoi

LAOS

Gulf of Tonkin

Hainan (CHINA)

Mekong River

Demilitarized Zone

Hue

THAILAND

Da Nang

CAMBODIA

SOUTH VIETNAM

Saigon

Gulf of Thailand

South China Sea

Saigon was the capital of South Vietnam. Hanoi was the North Vietnamese capital. After the war, the nation unified as the Socialist Republic of Vietnam, with Hanoi as the capital.

## U.S. Invasion

War broke out in 1954. The United States sent military advisers, guns, and ammunition to South Vietnam. U.S. officials feared that if the communists moved into South Vietnam, neighboring countries such as Laos, Cambodia, Thailand, and Indonesia would also fall.

## Gulf of Tonkin

U.S. involvement increased over time. On August 2, 1964, a U.S. Navy destroyer was attacked by North Vietnamese torpedo boats in the Gulf of Tonkin, off the coast of North Vietnam. Two days later, the destroyer and another ship reported that they were under attack again. Today, there is some question whether the ships were attacked at all. At the time, however, President Lyndon Johnson used the Gulf of Tonkin Incident to justify military action against the North. For the next 11 years, the United States fought in Vietnam. These are some of the greatest battles of that war.

U.S. helicopters played a major role in troop and supply transport throughout the Vietnam War.

# Operation Rolling Thunder

**President Lyndon Johnson was determined to show that he was not soft on communism.**

The "Big Belly" B-52s used in the Vietnam War could carry up to 51 bombs.

70162

## Back to the Stone Age

Some of Johnson's advisers argued for diplomacy. Others said that if South Vietnam became communist, all of Southeast Asia was likely to follow. Johnson hoped that if the United States flexed its military muscle, the North Vietnamese would back down and allow South Vietnam to remain a separate nation. Air Force Chief of Staff General Curtis LeMay and others wanted American planes to bomb the North "back to the Stone Age."

## Wings of War

Johnson approved LeMay's plan. On March 2, 1965, Operation Rolling Thunder began. U.S. bombers destroyed an ammunition depot just north of the **Demilitarized Zone**—the border between North and South Vietnam. At the same time, in a separate operation, American bombers pounded the **Ho Chi Minh Trail**, hoping to disrupt supplies from reaching the communists in the South.

## Plan of Attack

**U.S. Air Force**

| | |
|---|---|
| **Commander:** | General Curtis LeMay |
| **Tactics:** | Bomb North Vietnam |
| **Where:** | North Vietnam |
| **Date:** | March 1965–October 1968 |

Lyndon Johnson became the U.S. president after John F. Kennedy was assassinated in November 1963. Kennedy sent supplies and advisers to Vietnam, and Johnson added forces.

## Off-Limits

Operation Rolling Thunder continued for three years. Johnson picked many of the targets himself. U.S. warplanes destroyed bridges, factories, and other enemy sites. But the U.S. did not bomb Hanoi, the capital of North Vietnam, or the city of Haiphong, which had a huge harbor. Johnson did not want to destroy Soviet or Chinese ships there for fear that it would lead to World War III.

## A Failure

The Americans dropped more than a million pounds of bombs during Operation Rolling Thunder. However, the North built a network of bombproof tunnels. Every time the United States destroyed a target, the North Vietnamese rebuilt it.

Although some say Operation Rolling Thunder nearly crippled the North's ability to wage war, in the end it was a failure. Critics of Rolling Thunder say that the Air Force did not coordinate its mission with armed operations on the ground. The leaders of the North used Operation Rolling Thunder in anti-American publicity. They characterized the bombings as U.S. brutality against civilians. The bombing campaign showed the United States how a determined enemy could hold together under difficult circumstances.

U.S. bombs created a curtain of fire on the ground.

# Operation Starlite ★2

**With the rapid buildup of U.S. forces in South Vietnam, both sides were itching for battle.**

## Surprising the Enemy

By summer 1965, the Viet Cong—the communist guerillas in South Vietnam—had established several bases, including one on a peninsula near the South China Sea. The Viet Cong stationed thousands of soldiers at the base. They were massing to attack Marines at Chu Lai Air Base, located 50 miles west of Da Nang. The Marines organized Operation Starlite, the first major U.S. military campaign of the war, to prevent the Viet Cong from meeting their objective. A Viet Cong **deserter** told the Americans that an attack on the U.S. base at Chu Lai was going to happen soon. The Americans planned to surprise their attackers.

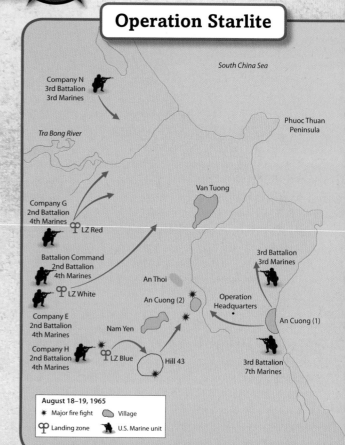

**Operation Starlite**

South China Sea

Company N
3rd Battalion
3rd Marines

Phuoc Thuan
Peninsula

Tra Bong River

Van Tuong

Company G
2nd Battalion
4th Marines

LZ Red

3rd Battalion
3rd Marines

Battalion Command
2nd Battalion
4th Marines

An Thoi

An Cuong (2)

Operation
Headquarters

LZ White

An Cuong (1)

Company E
2nd Battalion
4th Marines

Nam Yen

Company H
2nd Battalion
4th Marines

LZ Blue

Hill 43

3rd Battalion
7th Marines

**August 18–19, 1965**

| ✸ Major fire fight | 🔲 Village |
| ♈ Landing zone | 🔫 U.S. Marine unit |

## Coordinated Attack

Lieutenant General Lewis W. Walt drew up a plan involving U.S. air, ground, and naval units. Some Marines were to land in the battle area by helicopter, while other Marines were to storm ashore from the sea. Before the Marines were to land, Navy ships would pave the way with a massive bombardment of the helicopter landing zones.

## Plan of Attack

**U.S. Commander:** Lieutenant General Lewis W. Walt
**Tactics:** Surprise Viet Cong
**Where:** Van Tuong Peninsula
**Date:** August 1965

Helicopters evacuated casualties of Operation Starlite, covered by tanks and Marines with grenade launchers.

## The Battle Begins

The Marines launched the attack at 6:15 a.m., August 18, 1965. Navy ships began firing. Approximately 15 minutes later, the Marines landed on the beaches of the peninsula, just south of the Viet Cong positions. Other units followed, as U.S. warplanes pounded the enemy. One Marine battalion met heavy opposition, and at first it appeared that the Viet Cong would overrun the U.S. positions. But more Marines arrived by helicopter and trapped the enemy. The next day, several Marine units moved toward the sea, fighting off what remained of the Viet Cong units.

## First Victory

Fighting continued for a few more days. When the battle was over, both sides claimed victory, but losses favored the United States More than 600 Viet Cong were killed. The Marines lost 45 men, and 200 were wounded. Operation Starlite was the first win claimed by the United States. It boosted morale and set the tone for what followed. The Viet Cong would no longer battle the Marines again, unless fully supported by the North Vietnamese Army.

# Battle of Ia Drang Valley ③

Like the horse cavalry of earlier wars, helicopters could rapidly carry troops into combat. The U.S. air cavalry was first put to the test in November 1965. That's when the North attacked Ia Drang Province, in central South Vietnam. They hoped to split the country.

## Strong Enemy

U.S. General William Westmoreland, who commanded all U.S. forces in Vietnam, ordered the air cavalry into action. Led by Colonel Harold G. Moore, fighting began on November 14. The North Vietnamese Army (NVA) attacked just as Moore's men were getting off the helicopters. More than 1,000 other communist soldiers waited on nearby Chu Pong Mountain.

## Lost Platoon

Moore's men eventually left the landing zone and formed a defensive **perimeter** around a dry creek bed. One **platoon** went too far and became stranded. Additional U.S. troops arrived on helicopters as the isolated platoon took heavy fire. The NVA surrounded Moore's men. The fighting was brutal.

"Hal" Moore was first in his class at West Point to become a brigadier general.

## Plan of Attack

**U.S. Commander:** Colonel Harold G. Moore
**Tactics:** Stop the North Vietnamese from splitting South Vietnam
**Where:** Ia Drang Valley, South Vietnam
**Date:** November 1965

## Serious Trouble

Helicopter pilots braved enemy fire to bring in more ammunition and to ferry the wounded to safety. Just before dawn the next day, hundreds of NVA troops charged the south side of the American perimeter. The U.S. troops guarding that section of the line took heavy casualties. Then the NVA launched an even more aggressive attack.

Moore radioed for help. All available aircraft came to the rescue, which turned the tide of the battle.

Both sides learned lessons. The battle of Ia Drang taught the United States how to use its superior air power. The communists learned that if they waged a battle of **attrition**, they would be difficult to defeat.

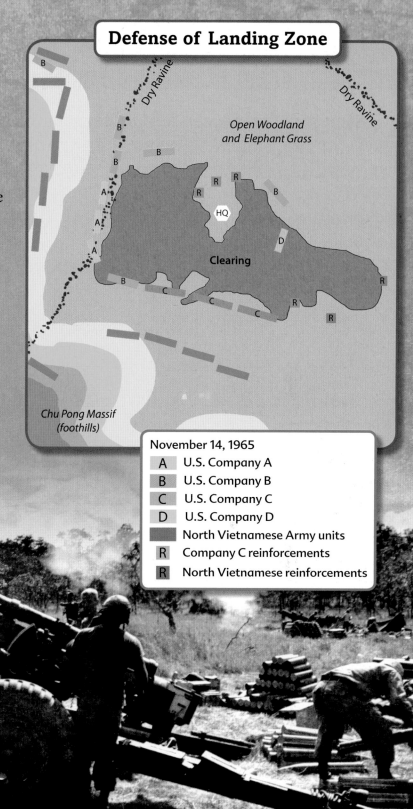

### Defense of Landing Zone

Dry Ravine

Dry Ravine

Open Woodland and Elephant Grass

HQ

Clearing

Chu Pong Massif (foothills)

November 14, 1965

| | |
|---|---|
| A | U.S. Company A |
| B | U.S. Company B |
| C | U.S. Company C |
| D | U.S. Company D |
| | North Vietnamese Army units |
| R | Company C reinforcements |
| R | North Vietnamese reinforcements |

U.S. artillery took aim at North Vietnamese fighters in the hills overlooking the Ia Drang Valley.

# Battle of Dak To

**Surrounded by ridges that arched to the mountaintops, Dak To sat in a valley near the borders of South Vietnam, Laos, and Cambodia.**

## Vanishing Enemy

In summer 1967, the North Vietnamese Army launched a series of attacks in the western Kontum Province. The United States sent troops to sweep the jungle-covered region. All was quiet by August. The NVA vanished into Cambodia and Laos. In late October, however, U.S. officials noticed that the enemy was moving troops to Dak To. Major General William R. Peers believed that the North wanted to start a fight that would cause the United States to send additional troops into the Dak To region. That would leave South Vietnam's cities and lowlands vulnerable to attack.

## Defensive Positions

On November 3, 1967, fighting began. The North was well prepared, as American troops quickly discovered. The communists had dug elaborate defensive positions on the hills and ridges around Dak To. According to some sources, 4,500 American troops faced 6,000 North Vietnamese during the campaign. Other sources say the NVA numbers were much higher.

The U.S. "Sky Soldiers" at Dak To were part of an airborne brigade that often fought without reinforcements.

## Plan of Attack

| | |
|---|---|
| **U.S. Commander:** | Major General William R. Peers |
| **Tactics:** | Defend Kontum Province |
| **Where:** | Dak To, South Vietnam |
| **Date:** | November 3–22, 1967 |

The soldiers in Dak To fought in the muddy hills, searching for the enemy.

## Hill 875

For three weeks, the Americans worked to dislodge the enemy. Each time the Americans located the enemy, they fired rockets and dropped bombs from planes. When the shelling stopped, the infantry moved in and fought. The NVA fought hard, too. They bloodied the Americans, then vanished into the jungle. One of the most savage battles began on November 19. On that day, members of the 503rd Airborne tried to take an area identified as Hill 875. At first they were successful, but the North Vietnamese ambushed and surrounded them.

## Elusive Enemy

On November 21, reinforcements arrived, and the 503rd attacked again. The fighting was savage, with hand-to-hand combat. Darkness forced the Americans to stop near the hill's summit. On November 22, artillery hammered the crest of the hill. The following day, the Americans moved up the mountain again, only to find that the North Vietnamese had left. The Battle of Dak To was a defeat for the North. However, the fighting accomplished one of the communists' main objectives: American troops began moving out of the cities and lowlands.

# Tet Offensive  ⭐ 5

By the end of 1967, many Americans believed the United States was winning the war in Vietnam. In reality, things were getting worse. The military had planned to have 525,000 U.S. troops in Vietnam by the middle of 1968. Both the military and the White House concluded that even more troops would be needed.

North Vietnam's Vo Nguyen Giap was a four-star general.

## Pressure for Progress

President Johnson placed a lot of pressure on the military to show results. The government provided misleading figures on the number of casualties and enemy soldiers. America's leaders did everything they could to squash doubt concerning progress in Vietnam. "We are making progress," Johnson said. "We are pleased with the results that we are getting. We are inflicting greater loses than we are taking."

Then the communists launched the Tet Offensive, which shocked the American public. On January 31, 1968, millions of Americans watched the nightly news in horror as U.S. Marines fended off an attack on the American embassy in Saigon, the capital of South Vietnam.

## Plan of Attack

**Communist Commander:** General Vo Nguyen Giap

**Tactics:** Attack major cities and military installations

**Where:** South Vietnam

**Date:** January–February 1968

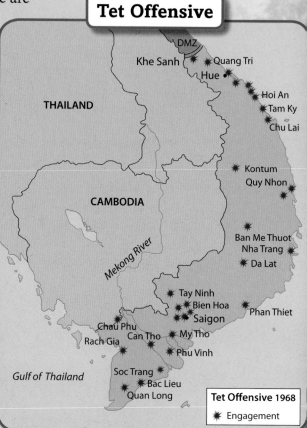

Tet Offensive

DMZ
Khe Sanh * Quang Tri
Hue
THAILAND
Hoi An
* Tam Ky
Chu Lai

Kontum
Quy Nhon
CAMBODIA

Ban Me Thuot
Nha Trang
Mekong River
* Da Lat

Tay Ninh
* Bien Hoa
Phan Thiet
Chau Phu
Saigon
Rach Gia  Can Tho * My Tho
Phu Vinh
Gulf of Thailand
Soc Trang
* Bac Lieu
Quan Long

**Tet Offensive 1968**
* Engagement

# Lunar New Year

The attack on the embassy was just one of a series of battles that occurred during Tet—the lunar new year. Tet is the most important holiday in Vietnam. Each year during the war, both sides agreed to a three-day truce. In 1968, however, North Vietnamese General Vo Nguyen Giap used the cease-fire to launch a series of surprise attacks against major cities and military bases throughout South Vietnam. Giap hoped the offensive would inspire the South Vietnamese to rebel against the government and join the communist fight.

Fighting began just after midnight. The Viet Cong and North Vietnamese Army overran the ancient city of Hue. They surrounded the U.S. Marine base at Khe Sanh. They also targeted coastal cities, such as Da Nang, which had been seemingly safe from combat. The communists assaulted General Westmoreland's headquarters at the Saigon airport.

During Tet, fighting raged at the U.S. embassy compound in Saigon.

## Embassy Under Siege

The most distressing scene was the battle waged inside the U.S. embassy in downtown Saigon. Nineteen Viet Cong commandos, armed with guns and explosives, blew a hole in the embassy wall and stormed the compound. With television cameras rolling, the Americans quickly killed the commandos. The firefight inside the embassy—a symbol of U.S. power—shocked the world. The communists also attacked the presidential palace and the headquarters of the South Vietnamese army.

## A Military Disaster

The Tet Offensive lasted four weeks. It was, in the end, a military failure for the North. The South Vietnamese did not rise up and overthrow their government as General Giap had hoped. In addition, the North lost thousands of soldiers it could not replace. According to some sources, nearly 4,000 U.S. troops died along with approximately 5,000 South Vietnamese. The battle devastated the Viet Cong.

Back in America, the images of war on TV and in the newspapers angered many Americans. President Johnson tried to liken Tet to rioting that had been occurring in the United States over civil rights and a downturn in the economy. "A few bandits can do that in any city," he declared. His words did not go over well.

Using barricades set up by the NVA, South Vietnamese defenders fought back in Saigon during the Tet Offensive.

## Tet's Last Casualty

The Tet Offensive was a major turning point in the war. Afterward, U.S. public support for the conflict dropped. Lyndon Johnson was also a casualty of the offensive. The Vietnam War consumed Johnson's presidency. He had wanted to do great things, such as stamping out U.S. poverty and hunger, with a program called the "Great Society." However, his handling of the war overshadowed it.

President Johnson listened intently to reports taped by his son-in-law, who was leading a military company in Vietnam. The photo was used by some to depict Johnson as defeated.

When the bridge over the Perfume River was blown apart, villagers escaped the fighting by boat.

## Stalemate

Johnson did not want to lose in Vietnam. But by 1968, the press was reporting that Vietnam had become a **stalemate** and that the United States could not win.

Even some presidential advisers told Johnson that sending more troops would do no good. Johnson's most trusted consultant, Secretary of Defense Robert McNamara, believed there was no way to win the war. A month after the Tet Offensive, Johnson shocked the nation when he said he had decided not to seek re-election.

# Battle of Hue 6

Located on the northeast coast of South Vietnam, on the Perfume River, Hue (pronounced "way") was a holy place. Ancient Buddhist temples and palaces dominated its skyline. During the Tet Offensive, Hue became the site of one of the bitterest battles of the war.

## Quick Capture

In the morning hours of January 30 and January 31, 1968, communist forces blazed through the city from three directions. Each met little resistance from the South Vietnamese forces stationed there. The communists quickly seized the center of town and ran up the Viet Cong flag atop the Citadel, an ancient fortress near the Imperial Palace. The Viet Cong were armed with a list of people who were enemies of communism. They went house to house, shooting or clubbing people to death.

## Urban Warfare

During the first day of battle, South Vietnamese tanks failed to oust the enemy. Eventually, U.S. Marines arrived and waged a brutal house-to-house fight with the communists. It was difficult. One soldier said: "We were accustomed to jungles and open rice fields, and now we would be fighting in a city."

## Plan of Attack

| | |
|---|---|
| **Tactics:** | Part of the Tet Offensive |
| **Where:** | Hue, South Vietnam |
| **Date:** | January–February 1968 |

## Marines Arrive

The Marines adapted to the conditions. They crossed the Perfume River aboard landing craft as the communists peppered the boats with gunfire. The Marines entered from the north and cautiously moved toward the Citadel. Burnt-out tanks and trucks were everywhere. Upturned automobiles smoldered.

As they moved slowly through Hue, the Marines encountered **booby traps** and sniper fire. Because Hue was an historic city, the Americans and South Vietnamese at first did not shell or bomb buildings. But the ban was lifted as the fighting continued. However, even then the U.S. planes could not be fully utilized, because it was the rainy season.

During the Battle of Hue, soldiers fought in the streets, taking cover where they could.

## The Citadel

Finally, Allied forces made their way to the Citadel. The battle raged for 10 days. Television news crews followed the soldiers. On February 24, South Vietnamese troops, many of whom grew up in Hue, ripped the Viet Cong flag fluttering from the top of one of the Citadel's towers. Not long after, the Americans and South Vietnamese captured the Imperial Palace at the center of the Citadel.

## Aftermath

About 220 U.S. Marines were casualties of the battle, along with approximately 450 South Vietnamese soldiers. Thousands of communist soldiers lost their lives. Although Hue was an Allied victory, the American public was bitter about it. This and other battles of the Tet Offensive hurt American support for the war.

U.S. troops and tanks closed in on the Citadel during the 1968 fighting.

# The Battle of Khe Sanh

**7**

Khe Sanh was a ruggedly beautiful area near the Laotian border in northwest South Vietnam. The region straddled Route 9, an old French road linking the Vietnamese coast to the market towns in Laos.

## Khe Shanh Expands

Earlier in the war, the United States had built a small **Special Forces** camp to recruit and train people who wanted to fight the communists. General William Westmoreland expanded the base with supplies and ammunition. His plan was to use the base, along with its airstrip, to launch attacks against communist hideouts in Laos. Westmoreland sent a U.S. Marine battalion to defend the camp.

## Remote Outpost

Khe Sanh became one of the most remote U.S. outposts in Vietnam. In summer 1967, the North Vietnamese Army began to build up its forces around Khe Sanh. General Vo Nguyen Giap placed his NVA infantry, artillery, and tank units nearby. In total, according to some estimates, about 40,000 NVA troops were breathing down the necks of the Marines. According to some reports, Westmoreland sent 6,000 more troops to bolster Khe Sanh's defenses. He drew up plans to bomb the NVA, in an action code-named Operation Niagara.

## Plan of Attack

| | |
|---|---|
| **Main Communist Commander:** | General Vo Nguyen Giap |
| **Tactics:** | Destroy the American base |
| **Where:** | Khe Shan, South Vietnam |
| **Date:** | January–April 1968 |

**20**

## Terror from Above

For weeks, the battle raged. During the day, nothing much happened. But at night, the NVA attacked with infantry and artillery. One day, more than 1,000 artillery shells slammed the base. The Americans decided the only way to protect Khe Sanh was to use massive airpower. Flying from their bases in Guam, a tiny island in the Pacific Ocean, B-52 bombers dropped more than 75,000 tons of explosives on communist troops over a nine-week period. They flew 50 strikes a day. Other U.S. aircraft blanketed the area with bombs and rockets. Finally, during the early morning hours of January 21, 1968, the NVA attacked. They tried but failed to overrun two hills north of the base. Later that morning, the communists shelled the town with a massive artillery bombardment.

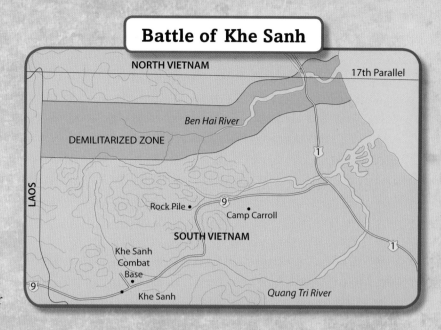

**Battle of Khe Sanh**

NORTH VIETNAM

17th Parallel

Ben Hai River

DEMILITARIZED ZONE

LAOS

Rock Pile •   9   • Camp Carroll

SOUTH VIETNAM

Khe Sanh Combat Base

9

Khe Sanh

Quang Tri River

1

## The North Scores

The NVA's mortars and rockets struck with deadly accuracy. One scored a direct hit on the base's main ammunition dump, destroying artillery and mortar rounds. Eighteen men died in the explosion, and another 40 were injured. The ammunition exploded for two days.

North Vietnamese guerilla fighters targeted the U.S. Marine base at Khe Sanh.

## Resupplying the Marines

The American troops also needed to be resupplied with ammunition, water, food, and other materials. According to one estimate, troops stationed at the main base needed 160 tons of supplies a day. The wounded needed to be evacuated. Huge C-130 Hercules transport planes flew in and out of Khe Sanh.

On February 11, the communists destroyed a C-130, killing its entire crew. It was the last large plane to land at Khe Sanh. Later, helicopters ferried supplies to the besieged Americans. The helicopters flew into the base protected by a massive artillery bombardment, fighter-bombers, and gunships.

## Taking Its Toll

President Johnson was worried about the Marines and their mission, and demanded the latest information. The siege was taking its toll on the Marines. They rationed food. At times, the men stood in their bunkers knee-deep in mud. Rats overran the base. Dozens of journalists were at Khe Sanh covering the gruesome story for newspapers, magazines, and television.

A U.S. officer and his scout dog inspected an enemy bunker southwest of Hoi An.

South Vietnamese villagers helped move the U.S. supplies.

## Military History

Many observers likened Khe Sanh to the Viet Minh's siege of the French army at Dien Bien Phu in 1954, which General Vo Nguyen Giap had also led. The French lost that battle and were thrown out of Vietnam. Johnson worried that the same thing would happen at Khe Sanh.

Meanwhile, the North Vietnamese Army dug miles of trenches at night, targeting the perimeter of the base, just as the Viet Minh did at Dien Bien Phu. American troops could not destroy the trenches until the B-52s dropped bombs within 1,200 yards of the American base.

## The Siege Ends

The NVA finally left after the destruction of the trenches. The siege of Khe Sanh lasted for 77 days. Just how many NVA troops died is not known. The Marines counted 1,602 enemy bodies, but some estimates put the total communist losses between 10,000 and 15,000. The Americans lost nearly 300 troops. More than 2,000 were wounded.

In June, the Americans destroyed their base at Khe Sanh. The siege, coupled with the other battles of the Tet Offensive, forced President Johnson to scale back American involvement in the war.

# Hamburger Hill

Ap Bia Mountain was also known as Dong Ap Bia. On U.S. Army maps, it was simply called Hill 937. The number indicated its height in meters. Today, it is known as Hamburger Hill.

## Apache Snow

Beginning in 1966, the A Shau Valley in northwest South Vietnam had become a major access point for communist forces traveling along the Ho Chi Minh Trail. The communists had seized an Allied base in the valley. Despite American attempts to dislodge them, the North Vietnamese were still there three years later.

The United States and South Vietnamese decided to destroy the fortification with Operation Apache Snow. On May 10, 1969, Colonel John Conmey's forces approached the base of Hill 937. The Americans and South Vietnamese planned to march into the valley, search for the enemy, and cut off the enemy's escape route to Laos just over a mile away.

## Friendly Fire

The hill itself had little tactical value. It was steep, heavily forested, and spiked with thick stands of bamboo. On May 10, U.S. forces searched nearby and met little resistance. The next day, a U.S. infantry force launched a **search-and-destroy** mission on the northwest ridge of Hill 937. Rather than retreat, the North Vietnamese stood and fought.

Over the next two days, the Americans launched a coordinated assault, but the mountain's terrain was difficult to overcome. They lost control. At one point, gunners in U.S. helicopters accidentally killed some of their own troops on the ground.

> Troopers from the 101st Airborne Division arrived by helicopter and charged up Hamburger Hill.

## Plan of Attack

**Main U.S. Commander:** Colonel John Conmey

**Tactics:** Destroy infiltration route

**Where:** Ap Bia Mountain, South Vietnam

**Date:** May 1969

Those who made it to the base camp waited for medical evacuation.

## Bloody Days

The battle for Hill 937 waged for 10 bloody days. U.S. troops assaulted the hill many times. Each time they were thrown back. Helicopters were useless because of the dense jungle. The North Vietnamese moved through an elaborate system of underground bunkers and trenches.

It didn't take long for American troops to figure out that repeated attacks on the hill were pointless. "There were lots of people who were going to refuse to go up again," one soldier said after the battle.

## Ultimate Worth

Eventually, the Americans reached the summit. When the fighting was over, 630 communists were counted as dead, although there is no telling how many more were actually killed. Approximately 72 Americans were killed and almost 400 wounded. A soldier nailed a cardboard sign to a tree that read, "HAMBURGER HILL." A second soldier added another sign: "Was it worth it?"

Many people did not think so. The day the Americans captured Hill 937, Senator Edward Kennedy denounced the operation as "senseless and irresponsible." A few days later, the Americans abandoned the hill, and the North Vietnamese reclaimed it.

After Hamburger Hill, the U.S. military decided to fight a defensive war, rather than an offensive one. They hoped to minimize casualties.

In 1969, Richard Nixon became president of the United States. At the time, he promised to withdraw U.S. forces from Vietnam. He said that as U.S. troops left the region, the South Vietnamese would take over the fighting.

## Operation Breakfast

Shortly after Nixon took office, General Creighton W. Abrams suggested that the president bomb Cambodia, a neutral nation that shared a border with South Vietnam. Abrams wanted to destroy North Vietnamese supply lines and bases. Abrams and others believed that North Vietnam was sending troops and supplies through Cambodia into South Vietnam.

In March 1969, Nixon ordered the bombing, which lasted 14 months. The first mission, called Operation Breakfast, began on March 18. During Operation Breakfast, nearly 50 B-52 bombers dropped thousands of tons of bombs. Nixon kept this air attack secret from Congress and the American people. It was the first of a dozen top-secret raids that went under the code name Operation Menu. During Operation Breakfast, American bombers dropped from 108,000 to 540,000 tons of bombs, killing between 100,000 to 500,000 Cambodian civilians.

## Plan of Attack

**U.S. Commander:** General Creighton W. Abrams
**Tactics:** Disrupt NVA supply lines
**Where:** Cambodia
**Date:** April–July 1970

A base called Frontier City was built near the Cambodia border in an attempt to slow action in the area.

## Bold Move

At the time, Cambodia was ruled by Prince Norodom Sihanouk. He had allowed the North Vietnamese to build bases in his country. However, in March 1970, General Lon Nol took control of the government while Sihanouk was out of the country.

Lon Nol was pro-American. Because of this, U.S. leaders saw an opening in which to defeat the 40,000 communists troops and destroy their bases in Cambodia. Nixon asked his advisers to come up with a plan to aid the new government. He sent his top adviser, Henry Kissinger, a memo: "We need a bold move in Cambodia to show that we stand with Lon Nol."

President Richard Nixon announced the invasion on television.

## Invasion

Nixon made an announcement to the nation on April 30, 1970. Standing in front of a map of Southeast Asia, Nixon said that he had ordered an invasion to destroy the enemy. At the same time, U.S. and South Vietnamese naval forces swept up the Mekong River to supply Cambodia's capital, Pnomh Penh.

A force of approximately 20,000 men, supported by U.S. warplanes, attacked two communist bases in Cambodia. The Americans thought they were attacking major communist headquarters, called the "Bamboo Pentagon," but found only a few empty huts. The enemy had left weeks before.

South Vietnamese vessels moved up the Mekong River toward Cambodia.

## Protests in the Streets

The invasion of Cambodia sparked sharp protests in the United States. Fueled with rage, the protesters, many of whom were college students, took to the streets and college campuses.

Nixon called the protesters "bums." However, many people disagreed with the president, including some government leaders. Around 200 U.S. State Department workers signed a public petition against Nixon's actions. Some of Kissinger's aides resigned their jobs in protest.

## Danger at Kent State

The outrage over the invasion reached its climax in Ohio at Kent State University. Students attacked and burned the Reserve Officer Training Corps building on campus. The military used the building to recruit college students. Ohio's governor, James Rhodes, ordered the National Guard to bring order to the campus. On May 4, 1970, some National Guardsmen fired into the crowd, killing four students.

The National Guard used tear gas on the student protesters at Kent State, in Ohio.

On May 9, 1970, a large anti-war demonstration was held in Washington, D.C.

## Give Peace a Chance

The killings sent shockwaves across the nation. More than 400 universities and colleges closed their doors as students and professors staged strikes. Nearly 100,000 people marched on Washington, D.C., surrounding the White House.

At a press conference on May 8, a reporter asked Nixon whether he was surprised by the intensity of the protests. "I know that what I have done will accomplish the goals that they want," Nixon answered. "It will shorten this war. It will reduce American casualties. It will allow us to go forward with our withdrawal program."

North Vietnamese captured in Cambodia were blindfolded before being sent to a prison camp.

## Aftermath

The military called the invasion a success. In reality, the invasion of Cambodia escalated the war. The only way Nixon could get the United States out of Vietnam was to negotiate a peace deal with the communists that contained significant concessions.

**By 1972, American troops were withdrawing from South Vietnam and handing over most combat operations to the South Vietnamese.**

## Massive Firepower

North Vietnamese General Giap decided to end the war once and for all. He planned a three-pronged invasion of South Vietnam using infantry supported by heavy artillery and tanks. One part of the invasion force crossed the border from Laos to strike at central South Vietnam. Another attacked north of Saigon.

The United States leaders knew the invasion was coming, but no one knew for certain where the North was going to strike. On March 30, 1972, the North Vietnamese crossed the Demilitarized Zone (DMZ) into South Vietnam. Additional troops moved in from Laos to support the assault. The Easter Offensive was under way.

## Plan of Attack

| | |
|---|---|
| **Communist Commander:** | General Vo Nguyen Giap |
| **Tactics:** | Destroy the enemy |
| **Where:** | Many locations across South Vietnam |
| **Date:** | March–October 1972 |

South Vietnamese soldiers pushed toward Quang Tri City in July 1972.

U.S. tanks took positions along the road to Quang Tri City.

## Holding Tough

Facing the North Vietnamese Army was a division of South Vietnamese troops. Many of the South Vietnamese were new to battle, yet they were able to stand their ground. On April 1, the North ordered a retreat. That same day, more communist troops moved out of the A Shau Valley and attacked a series of bases along the DMZ. The South Vietnamese counterattacked and battled the communists for three weeks.

Communist troops also attacked from Cambodia, targeting three South Vietnamese villages. At one of those villages, An Loc, the NVA surrounded the South Vietnamese. American airplanes came to the rescue and helped defeat the NVA.

## North Defeated

The North's Easter Offensive continued for several more weeks, but in the end it was a failure. They lost roughly 40,000 soldiers, while another 60,000 were missing or wounded. However, the communists continued to control about 10 percent of South Vietnam.

## The War Ends

In January 1973, North Vietnam, the United States, South Vietnam, and the Viet Cong signed a peace agreement in Paris. American agreed that U.S. soldiers would leave South Vietnam within 60 days. As for the North and South Vietnamese, they violated the terms of the treaty almost immediately. They battled for two more years. The war ended in a communist victory.

# Glossary

**attrition**—the act of wearing down the opposing side by inflicting casualties

**booby traps**—hidden devices designed to harm an enemy

**Cold War**—an ideological battle between democratic and communist nations

**communist**—one who follows the social and economic philosophy characterized by a classless society and the absence of private property

**Demilitarized Zone (DMZ)**—a military border, such as the one between North and South Vietnam created in 1954

**deserter**—a soldier who runs away from his or her unit

**guerilla**—one who conducts surprise attacks behind enemy lines

**Ho Chi Minh Trail**—the system of trails that formed a supply line for the North Vietnamese to the South

**perimeter**—the border of a military unit's position

**platoon**—a subdivision of a military company

**search-and-destroy**—a military tactic employed by U.S. troops in Vietnam in which small groups of soldiers were sent out to seek and kill the enemy

**Special Forces**—an elite group of U.S. troops, such as the Green Berets, who go out on special missions during war

**stalemate**—deadlock; a situation in which progress is not possible

**Viet Cong**—communist guerillas in South Vietnam

# Index